JP

ORCHARD BOOKS
96 Leonard Street, London EC2A 4XD
Orchard Books Australia
32/45-51 Huntley Street, Alexandria NSW 2015
1 84362 222 X
First published in Great Britain in 1998
This edition published in 2003
Illustrations © Penny Dann 1998
The right of Penny Dann to be identified as
the illustrator of this work has been asserted by her
in accordance with the Copyright, Designs and Patents Act, 1988.
A CIP catalogue record for this book is available from the British Library.
Printed in Italy

Old MacDonald had a farm

Penny Dann

little ORCHARD

Old MacDonald had a farm, E-*I*-E-*I*-O!

And on that farm he had a dog, *E-I-E-I-O!*
With a **woof**, **woof**, here,
and a **woof**, **woof**, there,

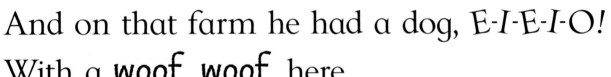

here a **woof**, there a **woof**,
everywhere a **woof**, **woof**.

Old MacDonald had a farm, E-I-E-I-O!

And on that farm he had a tractor, E-*I*-E-*I*-O!
With a **chug**, **chug**, here,
and a **chug**, **chug**, there,

here a **chug**, there a **chug**,
everywhere a **chug**, **chug**.

Old MacDonald had a farm, *E-I-E-I-O!*

And on that farm he had some sheep, *E-I-E-I-O!*
With a **baa**, **baa**, here,
and a **baa**, **baa**, there,

here a **baa**, there a **baa**,
everywhere a **baa**, **baa**.

Old MacDonald had a farm, *E-I-E-I-O!*

And on that farm he had some hens, E-*I*-E-*I*-O!
With a *cluck*, *cluck*, here,
and a *cluck*, *cluck*, there,

here a *cluck*, there a *cluck*,
everywhere a *cluck*, *cluck*.

Old MacDonald had a farm, E-*I*-E-*I*-O!

And on that farm he had some cows, E-*I*-E-*I*-O!
With a **moo**, **moo**, here,
and a **moo**, **moo**, there,

here a **moo**, there a **moo**,
everywhere a **moo**, **moo**.

Old MacDonald had a farm, *E-I-E-I-O!*

And on that farm he had some pigs, E-*I*-E-*I*-O!
With an **oink, oink**, here,
and an **oink, oink**, there,

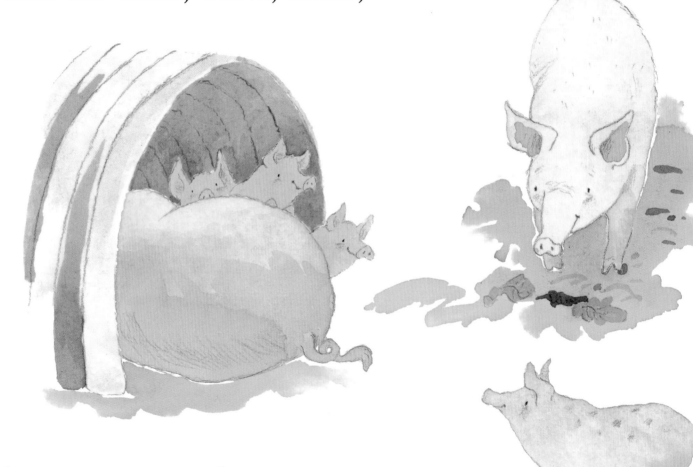

here an **oink**, there an **oink**,
everywhere an **oink, oink**.

Old MacDonald had a farm, E-*I*-E-*I*-O!

Old MacDonald had a farm, E-I-E-I-O!

With a **moo, moo** here

and a **baa, baa** there

an **oink, oink** here

and a *cluck, cluck* there

a **chug, chug** here

and a **woof, woof** there.

Old MacDonald had a farm, E-I-E-I-O!